Nicole M. Artz

FORTUNE TELLING

*How to reveal
the secrets of the future*

This book describes many tried and true methods of fortune telling handed down through the ages from one civilization to another and developed by master practitioners to a stage no longer difficult for the eager student to comprehend. It has been designed for the beginner who can choose to perfect one or all of the methods presented. Whether you decide to practice your newfound skills in a serious effort to develop psychic power or simply use them to entertain a party gathering is your choice. Either way, you will find yourself transformed with your highly sensitive perceptions and increased popularity.

METHODS THAT ARE OLD BUT TRUE

FAST AND NEW-AGE SYSTEMS TOO

MIX THEM UP AND TRY THEM OUT

DISCOVER WHAT IT'S ALL ABOUT.

FORTUNE TELLING

How to reveal
the secrets of the future

Hazel Whitaker

BARNES
&NOBLE
BOOKS
NEW YORK

CONTENTS

C O N T E N T S

ADVANCED FORTUNE TELLING

INTRODUCTION

THERE ARE MANY ASPECTS AND CHOICES OF FORTUNE TELLING. SOME ARE EASILY LEARNED AND CAN BE PRACTICED AT HOME, WHILE OTHERS ARE MORE ADVANCED METHODS WHICH REQUIRE LONG-TERM, IN-DEPTH STUDY AND A CONSULTATION WITH A REPUTABLE MASTER OF THE CRAFT.

This book will teach you the do-it-yourself practices of fortune telling, plus it will give you insight into the more advanced methods. You will soon have a favorite craft or you may prefer to indulge in all of the elementary methods. Whatever your personal choice, you may be sure that in taking the time to study the easy lessons in the following pages, you will have opened the door to psychic awareness, as well as mastering a number of crafts which will bring you pleasure.

Imagine, for example, the pleasant surprise your dinner guests will get when they discover that you are able to entertain them with your newfound skills.

Fortune telling is an enjoyable pastime which few people can resist. The only problem these practices will incur is the trouble you will have in persuading your guests to leave!

You will have fun selecting a new baby's name, or finding your lucky Lotto numbers with the help of numerology, or discovering how many children you will have by reading the palms of your hand. And a pleasant cup of tea or coffee becomes a new pastime when it is followed by a tea-leaf or coffee-bean reading.

Whether we choose to believe that life is what we make it or that everything is predestined and therefore cannot be changed, curiosity compels us to seek all the help we can get with the important choices and decisions we must make throughout life. Fortune telling has long been a favorite way for a great many people seeking direction on such important issues as love, finance, health and career.

DEVELOPING YOUR PSYCHIC POWERS

MEDITATION

All aspects of fortune telling contribute to the increased awareness of psychic power, but the advantages of meditation skills are immeasurable because they are the key to opening up and sharpening all the senses, including the sixth sense which, being the most elusive and mysterious of the senses, requires the calming, persuasive influence of peace the practice of meditation creates.

Many years ago when living in the fast lane was more the exception than the rule, it was easier to achieve meditation skills; but these days we have to train ourselves to regain what was once a natural ability.

People who live in a less active environment find it much easier to practice meditation, while the majority who must cope with the rat race are obliged to take time out to learn this wonderful skill. We must therefore respect the masters of meditation and commit to the lessons they teach.

Psychic development is a natural by-product of regular meditation exercises, therefore its importance cannot be underestimated. These exercises can be practiced in the privacy of your own home or alternatively in group meditation such as a psychic workshop.

This makes sense when you consider that the degree of positive peaceful energy generated from a collection of people is far in excess of that generated by a singular effort. Various methods of meditation are practiced in psychic workshops, most of which are positive and successful; but some groups, fortunately a minority, favor drug-induced methods of meditation — these I do not recommend.

Perhaps the main reason why meditation is such an essential ingredient to the development of psychic power, is in its ability to help us focus on only the positive influences of the six senses, and therefore open all the channels of awareness.

BASIC PSYCHOMETRY

Psychometry is the art of fortune telling by way of holding an object such as jewelry or clothing belonging to a person and meditating on the object until the psychometrist sees, feels, or hears past, present or future events connected to the object's owner. While this method of fortune telling requires much time and practice to reach an advanced stage, basic psychometry is relatively easy to learn.

Elementary psychometry is the practice of handling an object of jewelry belonging to a friend and noting the fragmented impressions for future reference. It is the early stages of learning this skill that require the most patience, because these first impressions will not always make sense at the time — progress and hindsight will provide clarification.

That is why it is important to make notes of all the impressions you receive. For instance, did you feel happy, sad, excited, or indifferent when you first handled the piece of jewelry? Did you experience a feeling of harmony, irritability, security or instability? Little things mean a lot more than you may think in these early stages.

To start, make a mental note of your first impressions when you next shake hands with someone and of the most impressionable feeling you have when you enter a person's home or a strange building. Before long, you will find yourself doing these automatically, and once it becomes known to your friends that you are capable of even the most basic psychometry skills, their curiosity will keep you busy and in practice. But remember, never upset or offend anyone with your predictions, even when you become experienced enough to have them. If you have nothing positive to report — don't report it. Remember you are a student psychometrist not a student psychiatrist.

PSYCHIC WORKSHOPS

Reputable psychic workshops, which teach you all the various means of fortune telling from an elementary to an advanced level, are not easy to locate. But, like any school of learning, it is worth the effort you put into finding the best to become the best.

The only prerequisites you need to join a psychic workshop are a mind free of restraints and a desire to contribute as much positive psychic energy as you desire to receive. These workshops are a team effort, so you need to believe in the motto: there is no "I" in team.

Collective psychic energy creates great power, and much good can come out of the meditative influences in a psychic circle. The intention of the workshops is for the students and teachers to combine their efforts and energies in the development of mutual psychic awareness.

Meditation, psychometry, palmistry, numerology, card reading, tea leaf and coffee bean reading are a few of the fortune telling skills you will learn to master. Creating the right atmosphere with music, color, chanting, and the burning of powerful but discrete aromatic essences and candles during a meditation period, will enhance individual and collective spiritual and psychic growth.

Psychic workshops create as many advantages and disadvantages as any other form of workplace, therefore you will not always have a completely compatible team. We live on a learning planet, so there are no perfect conditions or perfect beings. Life is a challenge, so we must strive to improve conditions and to improve our limitations. Psychic ability and fortune telling are a means by which we can achieve these goals. Throughout the world, regardless of creed or culture, people continue to seek the answers to their personal problems and look for solutions to life's adversities.

Psychic workshops do not have all the answers, but they do teach you how to develop the skills which contribute to these answers. The innately curious nature of human beings creates an insatiable appetite for the mystery surrounding the skills of fortune telling, hence the popularity of psychic workshops. These centers not only attract the genuine student, they are also vulnerable to attracting emotionally insecure people. These people become dependant on fortune telling to solve all their problems and this is not how it is supposed to be. They often forget to use logic and commonsense to run their day-to-day lives. This can then lead to self-obsession of the most unhealthy kind. At the end of the day, you are responsible for which choices you make in life.

There are also periods of time when, for your own sake, as well as the sake of your peers, it is wise to take a break from the workshop. Negative forces affect everyone at some time or another. For instance, if you are experiencing serious nervous disorders, or your attitude is bad due to illness or emotional upheaval, these periods can become times of self-pity and self-indulgence, and this is detrimental to team work. Perhaps you should become involved with some alternative recreation such as sport and lighthearted entertainment during these times. This way you will gradually recreate your psychic energy and can return to your psychic workshop activities with a new and positive attitude.

It is not uncommon to find some students chopping and changing psychic workshops and this disadvantages everyone. Consistency is an important ingredient in developing psychic ability, so unless you are experiencing difficulty because of incompatibility with your workshop peers, you should strive to be persistent and consistent.

FORTUNE TELLING
AT HOME

AUTOMATIC WRITING

Automatic writing requires patience, meditation, and a serene atmosphere in which to work. It may not be the most popular method of fortune telling, nor the easiest to master, but it is definitely a rewarding practice. Mood music, incense burning, subdued lighting and the gentle flicker of white candles, are all psychic-enhancing ingredients useful to this exercise. Choose your favorite writing paper and a special pen which you then keep solely for this purpose. Select a comfortable straight-backed chair and let all tension go by taking some deep breaths. Place the pen in a relaxed position in the hand and you are ready to begin.

During this meditation phase, it helps if you can focus on a particular subject: for instance, your career, love life, finances, or even some current world event that interests you at the time.

If you have chosen a person as the object of concentration, it would be advantageous if you place a photograph of him or her in front of you. Imagine that someone else is controlling the pen and guiding it in your hand, much like your parents once assisted you when they were teaching you to write. You may not be successful in getting a reaction in the first few attempts, but do not be disheartened. In time the pen will flow freely, and this level of automatic writing will be maintained.

The next step is to practice your newly developed skill on a friend who is present during the exercise. Before proceeding with the exercise of automatic writing, invite your friend to relax and enjoy the atmosphere you have created and to spend some time in quiet meditation with you.

At this point I should explain that in the early stages of your development, the automatic writing may be illegible and something of a scrawl — you may find part sentences, names and single words. At the time, they may make a lot of sense, but all of these messages should be recorded for further reference. When the pieces start to come together they, like a jigsaw, give a more detailed picture and a complete message should reveal itself. Thus your patience is rewarded.

Some students of this craft are surprised to find that instead of the written text they were expecting to see, they are confronted by a drawing of a person or place connected with the inquiry. A majority of students in this category go on to become psychic artists — in some cases, the first pictures they create turn out to be their spirit guides, who have been and will continue to be their inspiration and contact.

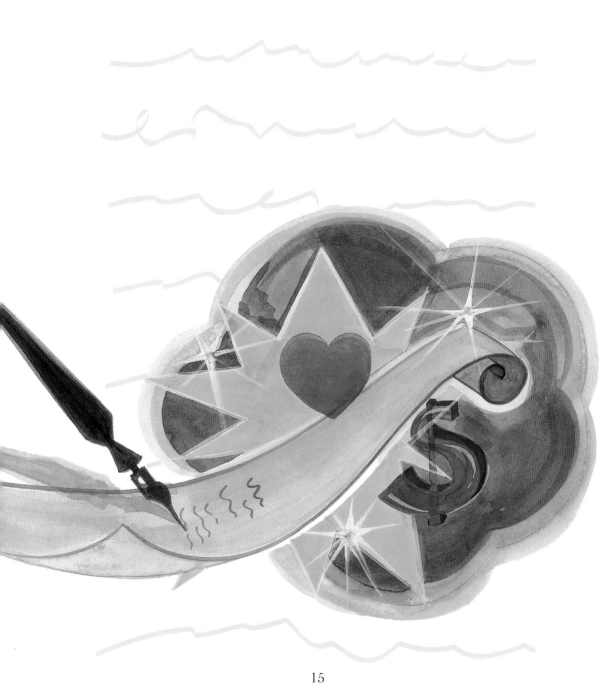

CRYSTAL BALL GAZING

Fortune telling by way of crystal ball gazing is another method that is best served by good meditation skills and the benefit of a psychic-enhancing environment.

The brightly turbaned gypsy lady, sitting in her tent surrounded by pictures of black cats and witches' brooms, conjures up visions of the typical fortune teller for many people, and a visit to her mysterious encampment is still a popular pastime.

More serious students and devotees of this method of fortune telling, however, prefer to consult the crystal ball in a still mysterious but more modern setting.

A good quality crystal ball is an expensive item, but it is a good investment because of its beautiful appearance and hardiness — and it need only be a once-in-a-lifetime purchase. It is a popular practice of fortune tellers to keep their crystal covered with a velvet cloth when it is not employed for consultations.

When you have created your psychic atmosphere, you are ready to begin. While meditating on your reasons for the consultation, place your hands around the crystal, without touching, and feel the energy surrounding it.

You will begin to have impressions about incidents relating to your inquiry. These impressions will take form as visions or symbols that appear within the crystal. By using this method of fortune telling you are employing and improving your clairvoyant skills. By the time you have mastered this craft, you will be receiving detailed and accurate accounts about events connected to the person whose destiny is being predicted.

Crystal ball gazing is a little like the silent movies — you see images that move but you don't hear anything. It is a pleasant and informative pastime as well as a serious method of fortune telling; however, since life is not always a barrel of laughs, you will occasionally see a picture predicting a sad occasion. Should you tell? If you need to ask yourself this question, then the answer is NO.

DICE

When the dice become instruments of fortune telling, it's a case of "short question, quick answer", which is why it is the fastest and easiest to learn method of divination.

The only other piece of equipment you need for this practice, apart from the three dice used for throwing, is a large piece of cardboard. Draw a circle in white chalk on the cardboard. The circle should be medium in size.

Evening is purported to be the most favorable time for this practice as it is traditionally the calmest part of the day. A superstition says that if you use this method of fortune telling during an electrical storm your predictions will be unreliable.

Method 1

Place the three dice into a small box or dish. Close your eyes. Make a wish. Then toss the dice onto the board. Dice that fall outside the circle should not be counted. Add up the number of dots on the remaining dice and interpret the total figure as shown in the following:

Three	*Imminent good luck and a wish fulfilled*
Four	*A slight setback will cause disappointment*
Five	*A stranger brings much new happiness*
Six	*A new blessing comes well disguised*
Seven	*You become the victim of gossip*
Eight	*Confusion causes unwise decisions — don't act in haste*
Nine	*Success in love and reconciliations*
Ten	*Success in career and finance is imminent*
Eleven	*Short-term illness causes you anxiety*
Twelve	*Seek advice regarding legal documents*
Thirteen	*Self-pity causes delays and hassles*
Fourteen	*A new social circle brings excitement*
Fifteen	*Follow your intuition about false friends*
Sixteen	*A short journey brings profit and pleasure*
Seventeen	*A stranger from overseas brings successful propositions*
Eighteen	*Happiness, financial success and a rise in status*

Method 2

For this second method of dice throwing for fortune telling, only two dice are used. Place the dice into a small box or bowl, and shake them well. At the same time, make a silent wish for a good future. Toss the dice onto a flat-topped surface and interpret the combination by referring to the table of meanings set out below.

Six six	*A period of general success starts with a financial gain*
Six five	*Your help with a charitable organization receives recognition and reward*
Six four	*Bitter dispute is resolved in a court of law*
Six three	*Short journey will end with an unexpected pleasant surprise*
Six two	*Someone gives you a gift which is unusual but useful*
Six one	*Emotional problems you are experiencing will soon be sorted out*
Five five	*A change of address and a new social circle is overdue*
Five four	*You will make a sizeable profit from a small investment*
Five three	*Unexpected visitors and happy reunions will surprise you*
Five two	*A friend discovers she is pregnant with twins*
Five one	*A fiery love affair suffers early burnout*
Four four	*Neighbors hold a noisy party and forget to invite you*
Four three	*You are borrowing sorrow from tomorrow — worrying about trivia*
Four two	*Beware of flattery from a handsome but fickle admirer*
Four one	*Finances take a dive, but only for a short period*
Three three	*Rivalry in your love life causes jealous outbursts*
Three two	*Don't gamble today unless you are prepared to lose*
Three one	*Someone else's misfortune makes you the beneficiary of success*
Two two	*A new love affair is the beginning of long-term happiness*
Two one	*An article of sentimental value is lost but will turn up later*
One one	*Important decisions made now will result in success*

I CHING

One of the Five Classics of Chinese antiquity, the I CHING or "Book of Changes" is an oracle that you can consult to guide you through every aspect of your life. While many people believe it to be a form of fortune telling, its purpose is to show you how to handle difficult situations, make wise decisions, and clarify the truth in the way of "the superior man". It can in this process give you at the very least some insight into the future should you follow a given path; sometimes the outcome will be so clear as to constitute a prediction in regard to the question you have asked.

The I CHING or Book of Changes is made up of 64 hexagrams that relate to all aspects of daily life. The hexagrams are attributed to the founder of the Chou dynasty, Wen Wang, in 12th-century B.C. Each hexagram has commentaries which are believed to have been written around 475–221 B.C.

The various translations take different forms, so when buying a copy check the others to see which you prefer. For instance, the James Legge translation separates the hexagrams and the commentaries, while the Richard Wilhelm translation puts the commentaries together with the hexagrams. Another difference between these two translations is that Legge did not translate the names of the hexagrams while Richard Wilhelm did — indeed, the English names given here are from the Wilhelm translation.

But whatever translation you choose, the concept is the same. The I CHING is concerned with the cycle of change caused by action and reaction and how an action you may take in regard to your question will affect your life. The oracle will show you the way of the "superior man" and warn against the ways of the "inferior man".

The Nature of the Oracle

When you throw the coins or count out the yarrow sticks seeking an answer to something, if you are sincere, the I CHING will try very hard to help you. If you are flippant, the I CHING will either give you a scolding if there is some merit hidden in your attitude or give you a hexagram that seems meaningless and completely off the point — the oracle will not be bothered by your tests or games. If you are not content with the answer the I CHING gives you, because it is not what you wanted to hear (the I CHING is more concerned with truth and honor than making you feel better), and continue to ask the same question again and again, you will no doubt get hexagram 4, *Meng* (Youthful Folly). Youthful Folly is very much the scolding parent and will make you blush.

The I CHING teaches you to consider the consequences of your actions and the way you think about things. It requires you to scrutinize your motives and attitudes, and to strive to strengthen your character. If you are behaving in a weak manner, the oracle will refer to "the inferior man".

If you wish to build your character and develop spiritually, then the I CHING will work wonders for you — before too long, you will find yourself thinking in the way of the I CHING. You will know instinctively the way of the superior man and the folly of the inferior man.

The Trigrams

The trigrams, which are formed by three lines, are at the basis of the ancient philosophy of China and are the building blocks of the I CHING. They are said to have been seen on the back of a tortoise by the legendary emperor Fu Hsi in the 24th century B.C.

CH'IEN	K'UN	CHEN	KEN	K'AN	LI	TUI	SUN
The Creative	the Receptive	the Arousing	Keeping Still	the Abysmal	the Clinging	the Joyous	the Gentle
Heaven	Earth	Thunder	Mountain	Water	Fire	Lake	Wood
Strong	Yielding	Movement	Standstill	Dangerous	Dependence	Pleasure	Penetrating
Horse	Cow	Dragon	Dog	Pig	Pheasant	Sheep	Cock

The Hexagrams

The hexagrams are a combination of any two of the trigrams. They are created by throwing three coins six times (or by the complex method of counting out yarrow stalks) while asking your question. With each throw you will get either 6, 8, 7, or 9; heads (*yin* or light principle) are worth 3 and tails (*yin* or dark principle) are worth 2, e.g., T+T+H=7. Write on a piece of paper your six lines, beginning at the bottom and working your way up, so that the lines take their correct positions. Unbroken lines (7 and 9) are *yang* or the light principle and broken lines (6 and 8) are *yin*, the dark principle.

To find out what hexagram you have you need to identify the lower and upper trigrams. In the case illustrated below, the first three lines form the lower trigram *K'un* and the next three lines form the upper trigram *Li*. Together they form hexagram 35, *Chin* which means Progress. If you get a 6 you put a cross on it, a 9, a circle. These are the changing lines, so-called because once you have read the hexagram, they turn into their opposites which create yet another hexagram — this represents either the future outcome of your question or a deeper insight into your situation.

When I was about to buy a particular house in an area remote from my friends, for that was all I could afford, I was extremely worried about how this would affect my life. I threw the coins six times and came up with hexagram 35, *Chin* (Progress). This then changed to hexagram 40 *Hsieh* (Deliverance).

Nine at the top	—o—	changes to	Six at the top	—x—
Eight in the fifth place	__ __		Eight in the fifth place	__ __
Seven in the fourth place	_____		Seven in the fourth place	_____
Eight in the third place	__ __		Eight in the third place	__ __
Six in the second place	__ __	changes to	Nine in the second place	—o—
Eight at the beginning	__ __		Eight in the beginning	__ __

It was clear even by the names of the hexagrams, Progress and Deliverance, that it would be very good for me to go ahead with buying the house. Much good luck has come my way since; as well, I have expanded creatively, personally, and spiritually.

Interpreting the Hexagram

The text of the I CHING is highly symbolic and can be very difficult to understand. It is important to realize that the interpretation of the imagery requires you to stretch your mind over the hexagram and let it float over the imagery without judgment to see how it affects your situation. For instance, hexagram 7, *Shih* (the Army) can refer to a group of many or few people that would benefit by operating in a manner similar to that of an army — this could mean your place of work, your theater group, your club, any group in fact that needs order, a leader, and loyalty and support in order to break through difficulties. This same hexagram could also be referring to your mind. If you are being overwhelmed by your problems, your mind could need ordering, and this hexagram shows you how to set your personal chaos in order.

The Miracle of the I CHING

For people who use the I CHING sincerely and on a regular basis, it does indeed seem to be the ultimate parent — all-knowing, all-wise, compassionate, and scolding. It seems to have genuine emotions and a forceful living presence. The I CHING will never let the sincere person down, even if he or she makes a mistake in putting the lines down. When I first began using the oracle 26 years ago, I was confused about which lines were broken and which were unbroken and whether they went from top to bottom or bottom to top. After I threw the coins and made up the hexagram, I realized that I had made a mistake in the order of the lines. I threw the coins again, making sure this time that I did it right, and I got the very same hexagram again with the same changing lines. Despite my errors, the I CHING knew what I was doing and gave me the correct hexagram anyway — several other people I know have had similar experiences. Westerners who use the I CHING know that it works and wonder how it does. Science has no explanation for it.

ALL THE HEXAGRAMS GIVE POWERFUL LESSONS.
THEY ARE WORTH READING EVEN IF YOU ARE NOT
ASKING A QUESTION.

NUMEROLOGY

The positive and negative influences that the power of numbers has on our personal destinies is vast and well documented. To practice the art of numerology — predicting the future with numbers — you do not need a good knowledge of mathematics. While this method of fortune telling is quite simple to practice, it is nonetheless an interesting and powerful way to discover important character traits about a person, enabling you to better understand him or her.

Numerology consists of many ways of revealing the past, present and future; however, the intention of this chapter is to furnish you with the essential basic skills required to discover your Personal Destiny Number, Personal Year Number, Lucky Lotto Numbers and how to discover your Name Number.

Once you have mastered the simple techniques outlined in the next few pages, you can use them to entertain your family and friends — they will be amazed.

An important point to remember is that while you follow the general method of reducing the addition of your Birth Number, your Personal Year Number, or your Name Number to a single digit, when you get eleven or twenty-two, you do not reduce these to a single digit, because these two numbers have a special power of their own.

Another interesting point to note is that although you cannot change your Destiny Number (because you cannot change the date of your birth) you can change your Name Number by changing the spelling of your name in order to get maximum benefit from a positive Name Number. Many celebrities have done so, with remarkable results.

No one's life is so perfect that it would not benefit from the insights numerology can give you.

Your Personal Year Number

Apart from the importance of your Destiny Number and your Name Number, each new year has a number of its own, e.g. 1998: 1 + 9 + 9 + 8 = 27 = 9. Hence, this year of 1998 is governed by the number nine whose qualities include humanitarianism, spirituality, and psychic evolvement — it is no coincidence that psychic awareness is becoming increasingly popular.

To calculate your Personal Year Number, follow these instructions: If your birthday is 1 February 1934, and the present year is 1998, you would replace 1934 with 1998: 1 + 2 + 1 + 9 + 9 + 8 = 30 = 3 + 0 = 3. Hence, your Personal Year Number for 1998 would be number three. If your birthday is 15 March 1972, change 1972 to 1998, this will then give you 1+5+3+1+9+9+8 = 36 3+6=9, therefore nine is your Personal Year Number — refer to the individual meanings of the numbers on pages 28–29 to discover the positive and negative influences affecting you for this year.

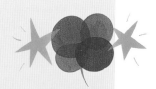

Your Lucky Lottery Numbers

How many times have you asked yourself: "I wonder which are my lucky numbers?" Here is your opportunity to calculate your personal lucky numbers and put them to the test for the current year. For the purpose of this exercise, we will suppose your name is Jimmy Smith. Using the graph on page 27, you then calculate the numbers of your name:

$$J\ I\ M M Y \qquad S\ M I T H$$
$$1+9+4+4+7 \ + \ 1+4+9+2+8$$
$$=25 \quad 2+5=\mathbf{7} \qquad =24 \quad 2+4=\mathbf{6}$$

$$6+7= \quad \mathbf{13}$$
$$1+3= \quad \mathbf{4}$$

The numbers in bold type plus your Destiny Number are your lucky numbers. You will notice that for the purpose of this exercise you are including the total numbers from your name, plus your Destiny Number — giving a total of seven numbers. It remains only for me to wish you good luck with your endeavors.

Destiny Number

You can quite easily calculate your Destiny Number by following the elementary procedure demonstrated below.

Write down the date of your birthday. For example, if you were born on 6 February 1970, you write down each number, then simply add all the single digits together:

$$6+2+1+9+7+0 = 25$$

Reduce the total

$$2+5 = 7$$

You now know that a person born on this date has a Destiny Number 7. Refer to the individual meanings of numbers on pages 28–29 to discover the positive and negative influences attached to the Destiny Number.

Name Number

To calculate the number of your name use the graph below, taking into account only those names by which you are known. If your name is James Smith, but you are more regularly known and addressed as Jimmy Smith, then that is the name that should be calculated.

1	2	3	4	5	6	7	8	9
A	B	C	D	E	F	G	H	I
J	K	L	M	N	O	P	Q	R
S	T	U	V	W	X	Y	Z	

Example

```
J I MMY   S M I T H
1+9+4+4+7 + 1+4+9+2+8
=25 2+5=7   =24 2+4=6
6+7=   13
1+3=   4
```

Therefore Jimmy Smith's new Name Number is Four. Refer to individual number meanings on pages 28–29 for character traits associated with the Number Four.

The Meanings of the Numbers

NUMBER ONE
is independent, and has organizational and leadership abilities.
Negative Traits: tunnel vision, selfishness.

NUMBER TWO
is kind, gentle, and has an approachable nature.
Negative Traits: timid and can be gullible or easily flattered.

NUMBER THREE
is versatile, creative, good-natured, and is multi-talented.
Negative Traits: attraction to hedonistic behavior.

NUMBER FOUR
is practical, stable, dependable, honest and trustworthy.
Negative traits: melancholy, stubbornness, overly serious nature.

NUMBER FIVE
is extroverted, energetic, resourceful and daring.
Negative traits: tendency to have too many irons in the fire,
a stressful personality.

NUMBER SIX
is romantic, creative, compassionate and family oriented.
Negative traits: can be supersensitive and overemotional.

NUMBER SEVEN
is intellectual, philosophical, imaginative and psychic.
Negative traits: can be impractical, secretive, unapproachable.

NUMBER EIGHT
is ambitious, tenacious, reliable, honest and trustworthy.
Negative traits: can be opinionated, impatient, intolerant.

NUMBER NINE
is humanitarian, creative, psychic, sensual, and has
healing abilities.
Negative traits: can be self-serving, possessive, volatile.

NUMBER ELEVEN
is concerned with spiritual evolvement. People with this
number have unusual destinies.
Negative traits: can be self-opinionated and vain.

NUMBER TWENTY TWO
has high ideals and goals, and is highly psychic.
Negative traits: can expect far too much from others,
and become tyrannical.

PALMISTRY

Palmistry has been a favorite method of fortune telling ever since the time of the ancient Hindus who are credited with its origin.

The lines, mounts, and various markings found on the palms of the hands seem to tell a story. It is about the journey on which we embark to travel life's highways and byways, gathering experience as we go. If you take the time to study the unique map etched out on the palms of your hands, you will discover not only the quality and length of your personal journey, but also advantageous routes and warning signs signaling the danger spots. Well-defined lines which are long and uninterrupted signify positive qualities connected with that line, whereas broken, weak lines indicate setbacks and disadvantages.

Well-developed mounts signify positive energy that comes from the planetary influences governing the mounts.

Familiarize yourself with the general meanings on the various markings on the palms of your hands, so that you can easily identify the good and bad luck omens attributed to them. Some lines and markings, such as the "children lines", are difficult to see without the aid of a good magnifying glass. The children lines can easily be confused with the vertical lines which are often found on the hands of a person with literary or journalistic skills. These lines run directly under the Mercury finger, whereas the marriage lines run diagonally across the outside of the palm ending under the Mercury finger. Children lines run vertically into or through the marriage lines. Deep children lines signify boys — faint children's lines signify girls.

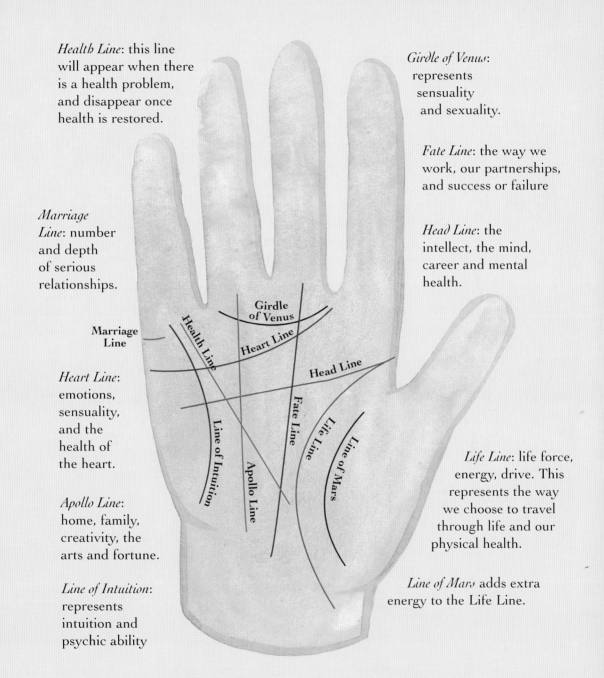

Health Line: this line will appear when there is a health problem, and disappear once health is restored.

Girdle of Venus: represents sensuality and sexuality.

Fate Line: the way we work, our partnerships, and success or failure

Marriage Line: number and depth of serious relationships.

Head Line: the intellect, the mind, career and mental health.

Marriage Line

Heart Line: emotions, sensuality, and the health of the heart.

Apollo Line: home, family, creativity, the arts and fortune.

Line of Intuition: represents intuition and psychic ability

Life Line: life force, energy, drive. This represents the way we choose to travel through life and our physical health.

Line of Mars adds extra energy to the Life Line.

Girdle of Venus

Health Line

Heart Line

Head Line

Fate Line

Life Line

Line of Intuition

Apollo Line

Line of Mars

The Mounts

The illustration on the opposite page demonstrates the names and positions of the mounts as they appear on the palm of the hand. Do not be concerned if these mounts are not well developed on the palm. It may be that the planetary influences attributed to them are evenly distributed and therefore do not appear to be significant. Not so — a well-balanced, focused personality often has palms like this. Similarly when all the mounts appear to be well developed, there is an abundance of energy flowing from all the planetary influences, suggesting a personality who enjoys life in excess — beware though, the result of this could be burn-out.

In keeping with the theory that palmistry illustrates a map of your journey through life, imagine the mounts as stockpiles containing the supplies essential to the success of that journey. For instance, how much more enjoyable will the journey be if Fate bestows an ample supply of qualities such as physical, emotional and sensual blessings? And should your journey be impaired by some ill-fated setback, would you not be grateful for the planetary influence that brings courage, resistance, resilience and bravery? Suddenly you realize you are equipped to meet the challenges of life.

It is up to you to make the most of the time you have to enjoy and complete the experience.

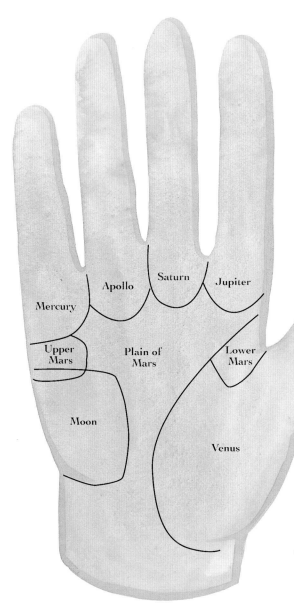

Mount of Jupiter: ambition, drive, willpower, religious beliefs, philosophies

Mount of Saturn: practical, material and scientific outlooks, dedication and responsibility

Mount of Apollo: home and family, and creativity

Mount of Mercury: communication, business acumen, honesty, literary and teaching skills

Mount of Venus: the home, family, love, stamina, sensuality and values

Mount of the Moon: the imagination, intuition, travel and freedom

Mount of Upper Mars: courage, resilience and temper

Mount of Lower Mars: military skills, resistance and bravery

Safety Signs and Warning Signals

Important markings such as the ones illustrated opposite will appear and disappear on the palms of the hand. They serve as temporary warning signs, or to herald periods of good fortune. Detecting the actual position of such markings is very important. Although, as a general rule, crosses represent some minor setback, it is important to understand the nature and cause of the setback. For example, if a cross were to appear on the life line, it could be signaling a period of loss of physical energy, because the life line represents the life-force. Whereas, should a cross appear on the head line, a period of mental fatigue would be a fair expectation.

Tiny red dots may appear on one of the main lines — they are difficult for the untrained eye to see, so you may need to use a good magnifying glass to detect them. They are cause for temporary concern. They are saying: stop — look — listen — avoid. Then, when the period of danger is over, they discretely disappear.

When one or more of the markings appear on any of the mounts the same warnings apply. For instance, if a cross were to appear on the Mount of Venus, a broken romance may be the cause. However, a square or star may also appear on this mount, which means that although there was an emotional setback, a new and exciting chapter, with plenty of good emotional vibrations, is imminent.

All the highs and lows we experience on our journey throughout life, are mapped out on the palms of the hand, and this makes palmistry so interesting and beneficial a skill to master.

Crosses	Crosses on parts of the palm will appear
	Whenever a time of trouble is near
Squares	Boxes or Squares are a sign of protection
	From danger which lurks from unwanted infection
Chains	Chains which have formed upon any line
	Are indicating a difficult time
Breaks	Breaks in a line of the palm indicate
	Short setbacks of a temporary state
Dots	Small Dots appearing need special attention
	These are a sign of Fate's intervention
Triangles	Signs of a Triangle signal despair
	Do not take chances, be wise and beware
Stars	A Star on the Mount of Apollo brings money
	Sometimes on Venus, a good-looking honey
Grilles	Grilles are quite simply lines in excess
	Excessive behavior leads to distress
Tassels	Lines that are tasseled mean energy drained
	When you overdo things there's nought to be gained
Branches or Forked Lines	Improvement is noted when Branches arise
	Drooping Branches can mean "sad surprise"
Islands	Problems and Islands are one and the same
	Did you create them? Or is Fate to blame?

PLAYING CARDS

Employing the use of an ordinary deck of playing cards to predict the past, present and future events of your destiny is an age-old custom that has proved to be both a popular and accurate method of fortune telling.

Students of the craft of cartomancy are immediately impressed by the easy technique of this aspect of divination, and professional readers continue to experiment and improve on a variety of creative ways of transforming the pictures and patterns of a layout into an accurate account of a person's destiny.

Each of the four suits (diamonds, clubs, hearts, spades) represents an aspect of life, and each individual card has a specific meaning. Groups and pairs of cards with the same numerical value are taken into account for their potential impact.

Cartomancy should be awarded the same respect as any other means of serious psychic divination. It is best practiced during the most potent period of the day, the early evening or twilight. This is generally regarded as the "bewitching hour", as it is believed the mysterious occult vibration peaks at this time.

All that remains is that you commit to memory the interpretations listed on the following pages.

The "7 Up" method, which means you use only those cards with a numerical value of seven or more plus the "Court" cards (Kings, Queens, Jacks) and the Ace, is easy and accurate and can be mastered in a reasonably short period of time.

YOURSELF

YOUR FAMILY

YOUR FRIENDS

WHAT YOU EXPECT

WHAT YOU DON'T
EXPECT

EXAMPLE

For this demonstration, the client shuffled the cards and asked for a general outlook for herself, family and friends over the next six months. Each position of this layout has a meaning. Once the client shuffled to her satisfaction, I placed one card face up in each position, and repeated the exercise two more times, then interpreted the combinations.

THE OUTCOME

The Meaning of the Suits

The suit of Hearts represents emotional issues: love and romance and family ties. The positive and negative influences that affect these aspects of life are examined by this suit. Hearts also represent the water signs, Cancer, Scorpio and Pisces.

The suit of Clubs represents communication, energy, environment, and the positive and negative influences affecting these aspects of life. Clubs also represent the fire signs, Aries, Leo and Sagittarius.

The suit of Diamonds represents the material world, i.e. money, business, and the positive and negative influences affecting these aspects of life. Diamonds also represent the earth signs, Taurus, Virgo and Capricorn.

The suit of Spades represents health both mental and physical, also the difficulties we must learn to deal with in life. Spades represent the air signs, Aquarius, Gemini and Libra.

Groups of Same Value in a Layout

ACES: 4 total success — 3 business negotiations — 2 marriage
KINGS: 4 reward for effort — 3 promotion — 2 minor reward
QUEENS: 4 gossip, slander — 3 idle gossip — 2 nosy neighbors
JACKS: 4 volatile arguments — 3 friction — 2 slight altercation
TENS: 4 good prospects — 3 serious money problems — 2 small financial gain
NINES: 4 great good fortune — 3 wish fulfilled — 2 pleasant surprise
EIGHTS: 4 anxiety, confusion — 3 worry, stress — 2 love affair
SEVENS: 4 public confrontation — 3 unexpected pregnancy — 2 lies, deceit

Individual Cards

A	HEARTS	Mutual love and happiness
K	HEARTS	A fair-complexioned, fair-minded adult male
Q	HEARTS	A fair-complexioned, affectionate female
J	HEARTS	An honest dependable young man
10	HEARTS	Success and good fortune
9	HEARTS	A wish fulfilled
8	HEARTS	An unexpected visit or present
7	HEARTS	A fickle admirer
A	CLUBS	Large investments you will wish to make
K	CLUBS	A kind-hearted man — dark-haired
Q	CLUBS	A friendly dark-haired woman who is inclined to gossip though not maliciously
J	CLUBS	Friendly young man with dark hair. Everyone's favourite but can be a rogue
10	CLUBS	Success in business
9	CLUBS	A large amount of money — sometimes a wealthy marriage
8	CLUBS	A small monetary gain
7	CLUBS	A dark-haired young girl who is friendly
A	DIAMONDS	New message indicating change
K	DIAMONDS	A man in a position of authority and power — fair or gray-haired
Q	DIAMONDS	A frivolous female. She takes what she wants — blonde
J	DIAMONDS	An official young man — someone in uniform
10	DIAMONDS	Change for the better connected with financial gain
9	DIAMONDS	New business deal
8	DIAMONDS	Work-related card; could mean a new job
7	DIAMONDS	An argument over money matters
A	SPADES	Great misfortune or even death
K	SPADES	A legal representative
Q	SPADES	Widowed or divorced woman
J	SPADES	An enemy — jealous and volatile
10	SPADES	Worry — vexation — sometimes illness
9	SPADES	Near fatal illness or accident
8	SPADES	Misfortune — danger — temptations
7	SPADES	Bad advice

SPELLS

The desire to enlist the services of magic spells in an effort to achieve your goals, e.g. snare a lover, get rich quick, or taste the sweet smell of revenge, is a temptation that few people can resist. The intentions of most of us, however, are not so much a case of greed or evil, but one of impatient longing for love and prosperity and a desire to expel enemies from our lives.

Every nation's history includes numerous accounts of folkloric beliefs and intense faith in ritual practices handed down from generation to generation. These practices have stood the test of time, spreading throughout the world and maintaining their popularity. Fortunately such grotesque rituals as those practiced by the lost civilization Maya are no longer required. Over the centuries humankind has turned to the mysterious wonders of nature's hidden formulas to evoke magical powers.

Many people still believe in the power of omens, talismans and amulets. We probably all know of at least one person who possesses a lucky mascot. Superstition is as rife as ever it was even as we hurl toward a new millenium.

I have chosen a few of my personal favorite magic spells that are easy to cast. Love, money and health are always favorite targets to work on.

Follow the instructions carefully — be mindful of what you wish for — and be sincere (you don't want to end up with a recipe for disaster). All the following spells should be cast after the sun has gone down.

Chill out

This spell is designed to put a distance between you and the person who is causing you distress: an ex-lover, a jealous rival, a nuisance neighbor.

Ingredients

A piece of his or her clothing (the more personal the better)
A lock of that person's hair
A photograph of him or her alone
A piece of paper bearing his or her signature
A deep freezer
A piece of paper, sprinkled with black pepper on which you write
down the words of the spell:

The chant

Wherever you go
I don't care a bit
You've messed up my life
So now you must split
Be quick and be gone
And leave me in peace
I do this because
This torture must cease

Procedure

✿ Cleanse your aura by sprinkling it with cold fresh (or blessed) water.
✿ Place all the ingredients in a well-sealed plastic bag.
✿ Place it in a corner of the freezer where it should remain until the problem has gone.

Honey-honey

This spell is designed to attract the attention of someone you love.

Ingredients

  A lock of his or her hair
  A lock from your own hair
  His or her signature
  Your own signature
  Some of his or her nail clippings
  Some of your own nail clippings
  A dead bee (preferably a queen bee)
  A jar of honey
  Sprig of honeysuckle
  Lavender oil
  One sheet writing paper
  Piece of red velvet material

The chant

  Honeysuckle, honey bee
  Cast your spell to work for me
  I am his (her) — he (she) is mine
  Stay sweet until our hearts entwine

Procedure

✡ Write the words on the sheet of paper.
✡ Sprinkle a little of the lavender oil over the words.
✡ Saturate the paper in honey.
✡ Place the hair, signatures, nail clippings, the bee and the sprig of
  honeysuckle on the honeyed paper (the ingredients will stick down nicely).
✡ Roll the paper up and wrap it neatly and tightly in the velvet cloth.
✡ Bury the article under your favorite tree or rose bush in your garden.

Smart money

This spell is designed to enhance your chances
of winning money.

Ingredients
 1 pomegranate
 1 apple
 1 orange
 1 avocado
 1 papaya
 1 chicken wishbone
 3 gold coins
 2 green candles
 Sugar
 Fruit should be over-ripe when it is bought.

The chant
 By the gentle light of candle glow
 I cast this spell to invoke the flow
 Of magic power enhancing wealth
 Bestowing luck upon myself
 So mote it be

Procedure
 ✿ Place the fruit into a glass fruit bowl where it remains untouched
     for seven days.
 ✿ Each night after sundown, light the candles, sprinkle sugar
     on the fruit and recite the chant above.
 ✿ On the seventh day (by which time the fruit should be off) stir the
     now soggy fruit with a wooden spoon and scoop the mixture,
     wishbone, three gold coins into an airtight glass container.
 ✿ Bury the container under the ground in a position close to
     the front door.

Get well soon

This spell is designed to improve your general health and should be repeated each night until the problem is removed.

Ingredients
One white and one blue candle
An incense-burner
A crystal bowl (fruit bowl) half-filled with water
The following essential oils: frankincense; myrrh,
    tea tree oil, lavender, lemongrass

The chant
In faith this aromatic spell
I cast to heal and make me well
Invoke therapeutic forces
From nature's universal sources
So mote it be

Procedure

✡ Sprinkle your aura with clear water from the crystal bowl.

✡ Play a CD of your favorite mood music.

✡ Light the candle.

✡ Into the incense burner put 2 tablespoons of water, 1 drop of frankincense and 1 drop of myrrh. Place a small candle into the burner and light it.

✡ Put one drop of each of the essential oils into the water in the crystal bowl.

✡ Place yourself comfortably cross-legged on the floor.

✡ Take some deep breaths, close your eyes, and sit in meditation while you soak in the peaceful, relaxing atmosphere.

✡ When you feel perfectly relaxed, chant the verse three times.

✡ Remain seated in meditation for the period of time that best suits your personal mood and comfort.

✡ Repeat this procedure each evening after sundown until the problem disappears.

TEA LEAF READING

MASTERING THE ART OF TEA LEAF READING NOT ONLY PROVIDES YOU WITH SKILLS OF INSIGHT AND DIVINATION, IT ALSO CREATES A PLEASANT AND ENTERTAINING PASTIME WITH WHICH TO IMPRESS YOUR FRIENDS AT THE END OF A DINNER PARTY.

The ceremony

If the best psychic or spiritual levels are to be achieved, tea leaf reading requires an atmosphere conducive to an easy flow of vibration. Most readers find that the leaves of China tea form the most easily read pictures, and it is essential to use a wide-rimmed, plain cup and saucer. Tea leaf readers prefer to use a round table or form a circle, in the middle of which they place a candle or incense burner to be lit during the ceremony.

Clients are then invited to sip the tea while thinking of the questions they wish answered. Before the cup is completely drained of liquid, when only the dredges are left, the client takes the cup in the left hand and turns it anticlockwise three times in a full circle, while silently making a wish. The cup is then turned upside down onto the saucer and left for a few minutes while the leaves dry out a little.

The procedure is complete and the interesting exercise of transforming the tea leaves into pictures and then into a story is ready to begin.

The reader takes the cup in the right hand and studies the patterns and pictures from all angles of the cup. Do not be alarmed or dismayed if as a student of the craft your first viewing appears as nothing more than dense or scattered masses of dried tea leaves — taking the extra time to take in the symbols and signs is well worth the effort. Take a few deep breaths and relax; enjoy the atmosphere and you will begin to see the transformation of the leaves into a picture story.

GOOD OMENS

Angels, acorns, anchors, birds, bees, bouquets, clover, corn, crown, cradle, dove, daffodil, duck, dice, elephant, eagle, egg, fish, flowers, fruit, garlands, gems, gifts, horseshoe, hands, heather, hearts, ingot, keys, lantern, magician, peacock, queen, rabbit, sun, stars, squares, calm sea, trumpet, trophy, university, unicorn.

BAD OMENS

Bat, black flag, clouds, coffin, cross, dagger, gun, monkey, mouse, mountains, moon, owl, rat, raven, scythe, skeleton, skull, sword, snake, tower, tears, teeth, wreath, wolf.

Predicting the timing of events as seen in the tea leaves or coffee beans is relatively simple if you consider that rarely does this method of fortune telling exceed a twelve-month span. The very top and rim of the cup represent the immediate future, the bottom of the cup represents events which will take twelve months to evolve, and the center of the cup represents six months.

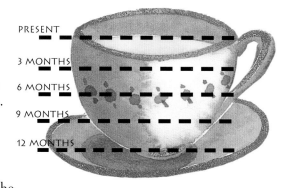

Some of the regular symbols which appear in the tea leaves and coffee beans:

Acorns   herald the good news that financial conditions are improving.

Angels   seem to appear whenever good tidings are due.

Arrows   symbolize unwelcome news — something needs urgent attention.

Bats   warn you to be aware of false friends.

Bees   represent a virtual hive of enjoyable activity.

Birds   are a sign of good luck, especially if they are flying.

Candles   show kindness and/or spirituality, especially if they appear to be alight.

Castles   denote the fulfillment of high ideals, goals and expectations.

Churches   represent solemn occasions, e.g. marriage, christening, funeral.

Daggers   predict secret enemies.

Dogs   represent good friends.

Doves   represent peace of mind and personal happiness.

Drums   represent noisy parties; also gossip.

Eagles   represent a position of authority, law, government, politics.

Eggs   that are well formed show good vibrations; cracked or broken, bad vibes.

Elephants   show good fortune — soon if the trunk is up — later if it is down.

Feathers   represent fragility regarding a physical or mental condition.

Fences   suggest you are imprisoned by your personal circumstances.

Flies represent minor setbacks.

Garlands represent honors that will be bestowed upon you.

Glasses suggest you are vulnerable to lies and deception; also false friends.

Guns mean that someone is gunning for you — but not literally.

Harps show that your quality of lifestyle is or will be of a high standard.

Hearts mean love, romance, marriage, happy results in emotional issues.

Jesters are practical jokers; frivolous actions.

Jockeys tell you to take a punt, because you are going to be lucky; a winning streak.

Keys mean a new experience; new doors open for you with pleasant surprises.

Kites tell you that you will rise through the ranks to a lofty position.

Lamps suggest that you will achieve a deeper understanding about your karmic lessons.

Logs are a heavy burden; they also represent stubbornness.

Masks mean you will be the victim of deception.

Moon full means a love affair; half represents marriage for material gain.

Numbers could be your lucky Lotto numbers.

Owls are not a good sign, contrary to popular belief — they means sickness.

Parcel suggests a luxurious lifestyle; vanity.

Rabbit represent timidity, phobias, fears.

Rainbow means protection and the assurance of a secure future.

Scales are dealings with the law that show a favorable outcome.

Ship means that at last your ship comes in; an abundance of good luck.

Table means a social gathering, a culinary feast.

Trees represent prosperity, growth, expansion.

Umbrella reassures you that you will be sheltered from adverse conditions.

Vulture warns that you will be the victim of envy and vulnerable to attack.

Wagon means transportation; you will purchase a new vehicle.

Windmill means that slowly but surely you will achieve success.

Wings are a messenger who brings good things.

THE TAROT

The Tarot cards consist of 78 Cards that are divided into two parts. Part one is called the Major Arcana and consists of 22 cards that are almost self-explanatory because they are well-illustrated and have descriptive titles. The Major Arcana can be used in the development of psychic and spiritual growth during meditation, and/or they can be used for fortune telling by interpreting the more practical meanings.

Part two of the Tarot consists of 56 cards which are divided into four suits. The Cups signify emotional issues and family ties, and represent the water signs of Cancer, Pisces and Scorpio. The Wands signify energy, communications and social issues, and represent the fire signs of Aries, Leo and Sagittarius. The Pentacles signify material and financial issues, and represent the earth signs of Taurus, Virgo and Capricorn. The Swords signify physical and mental health plus the difficult issues we face in life, and represent the air signs of Aquarius, Gemini and Libra.

Some experienced Tarot card readers prefer to employ only the Minor Arcana for the purpose of fortune telling because of the spiritual reverence attached to the Major Arcana. I do not agree with this theory because the spiritual and material worlds are interconnected. We live on a material planet, but while we are here, we are constantly learning through experience the Karmic lessons which promote the evolvement of our spirituality.

As a student of the Tarot, it is best to choose a simple layout (as illustrated opposite) to answer your questions. You will be surprised how much information is revealed in only 12 out of 78 cards. You can use the same layout over and over to ask as many questions as you wish. As a more advanced student you can extend and vary the layout. Eventually as a fully fledged master of the craft, you can use as many cards as you like for a single consultation.

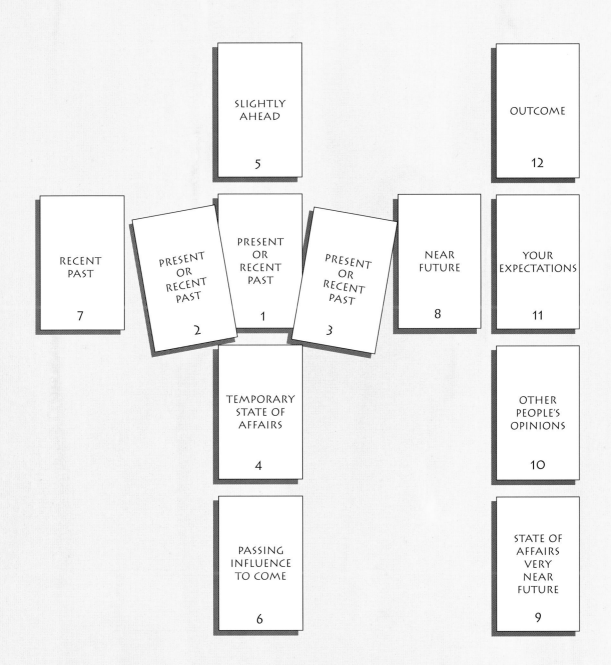

EXAMPLE READING OF THE FOOL

Obviously in a book this size I can only give you the essential meaning of each of the 78 cards in the Tarot pack, plus the meanings of each card reversed. However, to help you understand all there is to see in each card, and to encourage you to look for the deeper meanings, I have chosen the card of "The Fool" to demonstrate my interpretation.

No number has been assigned to the card of The Fool, because it represents the innocence and ignorance of our character as we enter this world. Instead it is called "0", because zero is the degree of knowledge we are born with — except for our intuitive skills, which can be denied or thwarted if they are not nourished.

Take a good look at the illustration of The Fool opposite. Notice how carefree his general attitude appears to be; ignorance is bliss for him, for he sees or knows no danger. Hence, this is a new experience for him which he anticipates will be an exciting experience. His brightly colored clothes represent his carefree attitude. He carries with him only a white rose (representing purity of thought) and a wooden staff with a brightly colored bag attached (representing the bundle of experiences which he will surely encounter). At his side is a white dog (man's best friend) which represents his conscience — the only thing he can depend on when he is alone to make his own decisions. No doubt the dog will bark or nip his heels when he is lost or making the wrong move — as indeed does our friend the conscience. Beautiful butterflies distract his attention (reminding him how fragile life can be) but the dog appears to be barking already, trying to tell him to stop and look before he leaps, for there is danger ahead. He is at the very edge of a steep cliff and will surely fall if he takes another step in the direction he is going. The choice is his alone. He may be hurt, but richer for the experience, or he can indulge himself in the fancy that every step has a silver lining.

When this card appears in a layout in the upright position it represents a new experience (a new look, a new career, a new environment, etc). Reversed, it represents a person who likes taking risks — one who will surely take that important step regardless of cost. This card in the reversed position is indicative of someone who insists on repeating his or her mistakes.

HOW TO PROCEED

The Tarot cards are potent and deserving of respect. Before and after use it is a good idea to carefully wrap your Tarot cards in a piece of black or purple velvet cloth, always returning the cards to their upright position so that they are ready for use again.

Spread the complete deck of seventy-eight cards — picture side down — on a table with an even surface. Commence mixing the cards on the table, making sure they thoroughly intermingle. Collect the entire deck together — picture side away from you. Now shuffle the cards the same way you would shuffle ordinary playing cards — but do not flick them. During this process, concentrate on the issues you wish to address; and it won't hurt to make a wish about something or someone special.

Now proceed to lay the cards out as per the illustration on page 51 and interpret them by referring to the individual meanings of the cards on pages 56–67. This layout is an excellent choice both for the novice as well as the expert because it is an easy question and answer method.

Always check the surrounding cards to establish the right context. For example, if you have The Empress in your layout, which represents fertility, pregnancy, motherhood, but also refers to the growth of nature or industry or whatever, you need to check the other cards to see which of these alternatives is relevant to your reading — obviously if the reading is about business, then pregnancy is an unlikely interpretation for this card.

Sometimes the cards will seem to be contradicting themselves. For instance, you may see the Ace of Cups in the layout (a great deal of personal happiness) which may be followed by The Moon (a card of fear, doubt, confusion) — but do not be alarmed, you will soon learn to interconnect the meanings. In this particular case the message would be that, though you fear disappointment, you need not worry, because the Ace of Cups has already promised happiness and it will deliver — the cards do not lie.

BASIC MEANINGS OF THE MAJOR ARCANA

O THE FOOL UPRIGHT: You are about to embark on a new experience. Don't forget to look before you leap.
Reversed: You are making a habit of repeating the same mistakes over and over.

I THE MAGICIAN UPRIGHT: A brilliant person, who is a specialist in his or her field. Often associated with the medical profession.
Reversed: The abuse or waste of a superior talent.

II THE HIGH PRIESTESS UPRIGHT: A highly intuitive female capable of great psychic power.
Reversed: Misguided psychic talent.

III THE EMPRESS UPRIGHT: Fertility, growth, expansion. Also predominantly feminine qualities .
Reversed: Infertility; sometimes a miscarriage; or someone confused about their sexuality.

IV THE EMPEROR UPRIGHT: A well-respected man in a position of power and authority.
Reversed: The abuse of authority; a control freak.

V THE HIEROPHANT UPRIGHT: Conservative, traditional beliefs, e.g. marriage. Respect for discipline.
Reversed: Unconventional thinking; rebellion towards tradition.

VI THE LOVERS UPRIGHT Mutual love; a well-matched couple; also a card of choice.
Reversed: Confusion about the choices in one's love life.

VII THE CHARIOT UPRIGHT: A good feeling about having control of your life; also represents a vehicle.
Reversed: Things are out of control in your life; you need self-discipline; also car accidents.

VIII STRENGTH UPRIGHT: Emotional nature; physical and mental strength; you can achieve anything.
Reversed: Weakness of a physical or mental nature.

IX THE HERMIT UPRIGHT: "Seek and ye shall find" a material or spiritual object or desire.
Reversed: You feel alone and lost, also lost property.

X WHEEL OF FORTUNE UPRIGHT: The wheel of fortune spins in your favor at this time.
Reversed: Some days you just can't win.

XI JUSTICE UPRIGHT: A fair and just outcome to a problem, also represents a well-balanced personality.
Reversed: An unjust outcome; you are being treated unfairly.

XII THE HANGED MAN UPRIGHT: A reversal of fortune — good or bad.
Reversed: Self-sacrifice; martyrdom.

XIII DEATH UPRIGHT: A sudden dramatic change of fortune, totally unexpected.
Reversed: The slow, drawn-out recovery of a difficult situation.

XIV TEMPERANCE UPRIGHT: Things will go well for you — the forces around you are blending together; good communications.
Reversed: Turbulence; uneasiness; bad timing.

XV THE DEVIL UPRIGHT: Temptation visits all of us from time to time. Remember, all things in moderation.
Reversed: Over-indulgence; hedonistic behavior. Don't forget a price has to be paid.

XVI THE TOWER UPRIGHT: Sudden catastrophe; danger — don't take risks at this time.
Reversed: Sometimes you are your own worst enemy, don't indulge in self-destructive behavior.

XVII THE STAR UPRIGHT: Your brightest hopes and wishes will be fulfilled and the gods are on your side.
Reversed: Your hopes and dreams will be delayed but not abandoned.

XVIII THE MOON UPRIGHT: Fears and phobias are causing you to doubt yourself.
Reversed: Nervous breakdowns; mental disorders.

XIX THE SUN UPRIGHT: Everything is growing and expanding; there are celebrations ahead.
Reversed: You must wait a little longer to enjoy the fruits of your labor.

XX JUDGEMENT UPRIGHT: You may be called for jury duty or as a witness.
Reversed: You will be the victim of poor judgment.

XXI THE WORLD UPRIGHT: Reward for completing a task.
Reversed: Uunfinished business.

INDIVIDUAL MEANINGS OF CARDS IN MINOR ARCANA

The Cups

Cups represent the emotional issues good and bad. Family matters. Love and romance in all its positive and negative forms.

ACE UPRIGHT: Peace of mind and personal happiness.
Reversed: Disappointments; disruptive influences.

TWO UPRIGHT: Commitment; engagement; bonding.
Reversed: Broken promises; broken romance.

THREE UPRIGHT: Pregnancy, which is a welcomed addition to the family.
Reversed: False pregnancy; miscarriage.

FOUR UPRIGHT: Refusal to accept a potential cup of happiness from the hand of Fate; fear of disappointment.
Reversed: Inability to forget past disappointments; refusing to move on.

FIVE UPRIGHT: Worried that love will pass you by; feeling unloved.
Reversed: You begin to take a chance on love again.

SIX UPRIGHT: Love of children; happy memories of childhood.
Reversed: Constantly living in the past; sometimes reunion with long lost friends or family.

SEVEN UPRIGHT: A card of choice; several opportunities present themselves; time to prioritize.
Reversed: Missed opportunities because of indecision.

EIGHT UPRIGHT: Temptation to pursue temporary distractions even though all is well at home.
Reversed: Putting emotional security at risk, believing the grass to be greener on the other side of the fence.

NINE UPRIGHT: Emotional contentment; the satisfaction of knowing your brightest dreams will be fulfilled.
Reversed: You may be in danger of becoming complacent because all is going so well.

TEN UPRIGHT: Ideal family condition, e.g. the right partner, healthy children, emotional security.
Reversed: Disruptions within the family; temporary setbacks that require the family to pull together.

PAGE UPRIGHT: This card has a dual meaning: sometimes it represents a new opportunity but it can also represent a female child.
Reversed: A missed opportunity or a boy child.

KNIGHT UPRIGHT: A single young man (water sign) looking for adventure.
Reversed: This same young man has become fickle and unreliable.

QUEEN UPRIGHT: Fair-haired lady, gentle-natured, kind-hearted, usually married or attached (water sign) .
Reversed: This same lady is now restless, easily bored, looking for excitement.

KING UPRIGHT: Fair-haired, blue-eyed mature man, good-natured, a hard worker, family-oriented, usually married or attached (water sign).
Reversed: He has now become possessive and overbearing and prone to selfishness.

THE WANDS

Wands represent communication, energy, the life-force, social issues.

ACE UPRIGHT: good news; a new beginning; the birth of a baby.
Reversed: Delays; hassles; teething problems with new ventures.

TWO UPRIGHT: A person who feels in control of all he or she surveys; new property owner.
Reversed: A potentially good property transaction goes wrong.

THREE UPRIGHT: Overseas trading; successful because of this person's capacity to know a good thing when he or she sees it.
Reversed: Overzealousness causes rash decisions with overseas trading.

FOUR UPRIGHT: Celebration of security; purchase of a high-rise building; sometimes represents an outdoor wedding.
Reversed: Postponement of a celebration due to unexpected setbacks.

FIVE UPRIGHT: Arguments, fighting, struggles and inner turmoil due to misunderstandings.
Reversed: An explosive situation comes to a head and may result in violent action.

SIX UPRIGHT: Success and triumph; victory. Reward for hard work.
Reversed: Lack of appreciation; unrewarded effort.

SEVEN UPRIGHT: Advantage; gain; success over adversity.
Reversed: Disadvantage; loss; victim of circumstances beyond your control.

EIGHT UPRIGHT: Speed; action; movement. A flying start to a new project.
Reversed: More haste, less speed is an appropriate warning for new ventures.

NINE UPRIGHT: Represents a person who is always guarding and double checking his or her security, but he or she can be assured of its safety.
Reversed: A valid feeling of insecurity because this person has none.

TEN UPRIGHT: Pressure; stress; burdens. Carrying a heavy load; problems with excess body fat.
Reversed: Weight loss; easing of pressure and stressful situations.

PAGE UPRIGHT: Female child; start of new but small project.
Reversed: Male child; short-term delays to new projects.

KNIGHT UPRIGHT: A young man (fire sign) unattached, brown hair, hazel eyes, lots of charisma, honest, trustworthy, fun loving.
Reversed: He is too popular for his own good and has become a lovable rogue.

QUEEN UPRIGHT: Mature-minded female, brunette, hazel eyes. Loyal, dependable, good wife and partner, loving caring mother, but a chatterbox.
Reversed: Jealous possessive female who tends to gossip a lot but is not vindictive.

KING UPRIGHT: A kind, warm-hearted mature man with brown hair and hazel eyes. Down to earth, honest, makes an excellent friend to both sexes. Hard worker who loves routine. Very approachable nature (fire sign).
Reversed: Practical joker, likes attention, flirtatious but not sleazy.

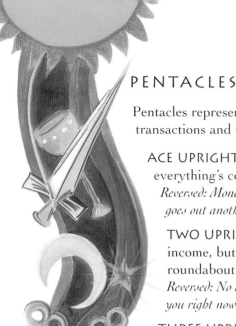

PENTACLES

Pentacles represent the material world, finance, business transactions and the effect these things have on our lives.

ACE UPRIGHT: Fate will hand you a financial gain; everything's coming up roses in your material world right now.
Reversed: Money keeps on coming in - but it comes in one door and goes out another.

TWO UPRIGHT: Financial turbulence has you juggling the income, but what you lose on the swings, you gain on the roundabout.
Reversed: No amount of financial wizardry seems to be working for you right now.

THREE UPRIGHT: Material recognition and reward for a job well done.
Reversed: You are being underpaid and overworked.

FOUR UPRIGHT: This card represents a person who knows the value of money and how to invest it.
Reversed: You are becoming a miser; it's a good idea to hold on to what you've got but you can't take it with you when you're gone.

FIVE UPRIGHT: Temporary loss of income, therefore decline in lifestyle and self-respect.
Reversed: Long-term unemployment and loss of income. You may need assistance from a charitable or welfare society.

SIX UPRIGHT: You will be in a position of being able to assist others financially.
Reversed: Your generosity will be taken advantage of.

SEVEN UPRIGHT: A slow but steady rise in income. You can now start a new savings account.
Reversed: Your meager bank account is constantly being attacked. It's in the bank one day and out the next.

EIGHT UPRIGHT: This card represents the apprentice; we all have to start somewhere; you only get out what you put in; new job.
Reversed: What seemed like a good opportunity soon collapses, pick yourself up, dust yourself down, and be prepared to try again.

NINE UPRIGHT: The luxuries of life are at your fingertips; it is a time of opulence; you can celebrate the fruits of your labor.
Reversed: A lack of respect for wealth can lead to hedonistic behavior.

TEN UPRIGHT: This card represents a family business which thrives and ensures that the family fortune remains intact for future generations.
Reversed: Friction; arguments; discord over the family fortune may cause it to be lost.

PAGE UPRIGHT: Dark-haired intelligent female child; a golden opportunity is recognized and seized upon.
Reversed: Dark-haired intelligent male child; lost opportunity.

KNIGHT UPRIGHT: dark-haired intelligent single young man who is down-to-earth, uncomplicated, and focused (earth sign).
Reversed: He is now arrogant, has tunnel vision, and thinks he's always right.

QUEEN UPRIGHT: Dark-haired mature-minded female, honest, reliable. One who appreciates the material world she lives in (earth sign).
Reversed: Dark-haired mature-minded female who is cynical and does not suffer fools easily (earth sign).

KING UPRIGHT: Dark-haired mature man, confident, intelligent, practical, well respected (earth sign).
Reversed: Dark-haired mature man, self-righteous, judgmental, intolerant (earth sign).

SWORDS

Swords represent the more serious and difficult issues we face in life. Sometimes life bites back at us and we must deal with it.

ACE UPRIGHT: The hand of Fate forces a decision that brings victory; success.
Reversed: Poor decisions or reluctance to make an important one proves to be disastrous.

TWO UPRIGHT: A truce must be called about a situation which cannot be solved any other way.
Reversed: Stubbornness, there is none so blind as those who refuse to see.

THREE UPRIGHT: Heartache; heartbreak; broken romance (sometimes physical heart problems).
Reversed: Broken romance; heartache is taking a long time to heal.

FOUR UPRIGHT: Urgent need for rest; a hospital bed.
Reversed: Forced confinement.

FIVE UPRIGHT: Battle (emotional or physical) fought and won.
Reversed: Battle against adversities fought and lost.

SIX UPRIGHT: Serious effort to escape turbulent times for the sake of peace of mind and a more tranquil environment; refugees.
Reversed: An unsuccessful attempt to escape difficult circumstances.

SEVEN UPRIGHT: Thief or traitor in the camp who goes undetected.
Reversed: The thief or traitor will be caught in the act.

EIGHT UPRIGHT: Imprisoned circumstances; a feeling of complete helplessness.
Reversed: Break away from restrictions and confinement.

NINE UPRIGHT: Migraine headaches; nervous disorders; a breakdown; deep depression.
Reversed: Slow recovery from the above conditions.

TEN UPRIGHT: Physical abuse; backstabbing of the worst kind; violence.
Reversed: Slow recovery from the above conditions.

PAGE UPRIGHT: Female child who is moody and has a secretive nature. Can also refer to investigations of a secretive nature and spying.
Reversed: Male child who is moody and has a secretive nature. Can also refer to a sickness that is difficult to diagnose.

KNIGHT UPRIGHT: Young man, olive complexion, dark hair who loves adventure, speed, a risk taker (air sign).
Reversed: Dark-haired young man who is out of control and dangerous to himself and others.

QUEEN UPRIGHT: Mature female who is accustomed to adversity and is not afraid to confront difficult issues. She has also been unlucky in love (air sign).
Reversed: She has become bitter and hardened because of repeated letdowns (air sign).

KING UPRIGHT: Mature man in a position of authority, legal eagle, politician. Confrontational but fair-minded (air sign).
Reversed: He is likely to abuse his position of authority and become tyrannical.

GROUPS OF CARDS

If two or more cards of the same value turn up in a single layout, they have a meaning of their own. The following list will provide you with the relevant meanings:

KINGS

Four: Complete success with all endeavors over the next three months.

Three: Success with a particular business transaction.

Two: Small promotion.

QUEENS

Four: Gossip or slander of which you are the victim.

Three: You will participate in idle gossip.

Two: Short-lived trouble with a female friend.

KNIGHTS

Four: Verbal and physical violence; extreme abuse.

Three: Heated arguments.

Two: Mixed messages or signals cause you to doubt the sincerity of a male friend.

PAGES

Four: Serious illness over a long-term period.

Three: Serious car accident.

Two: Short-term illness.

TENS

Four: Good to great financial fortune — a lucky time.

Three: Arguments over a money matter.

Two: Career change for the better.

NINE

Four: Your brightest hopes, dreams and wishes will be fulfilled.

Three: Good luck and/or a surprise windfall.

Two: Change of address.

EIGHT
Four: Confusion, confrontation caused by forces beyond your control.
Three: Anxiety; delays; hassles.
Two: Slight concern about a new romance.

SEVEN
Four: Serious misunderstandings; verbal abuse.
Three: Pregnancy.
Two: False friend.

SIX
Four: Emotional security.
Three: Exciting romantic time ahead.
Two: Justifiable faith and trust in your partner.

FIVE
Four: Travel; change; an energetic period.
Three: A warning not to overexert yourself.
Two: New experience.

FOUR
Four: Extreme boredom and a feeling of being imprisoned by your circumstances.
Three: You are being overly cautious about everything.
Two: A safe and secure period.

THREE
Four: Celebrations; the birth of a child.
Three: Unexpected good luck.
Two: Small but pleasant surprise.

TWO
Four: Looking in all the wrong places for love.
Three: Extra-marital affair.
Two: A commitment or an engagement.

ACES
Four: The best fortune in your finances and/or career.
Three: Legal action about a financial matter.
Two: A wedding.

ADVANCED FORTUNE TELLING

ASTROLOGY

Many people have the misguided impression that astrology is a fairly simple craft to master. In all probability, the most celebrated astrologers of modern times are partially responsible for this.

Every magazine and newspaper seems to have its own personal astrologer who predicts events for the day/week/month/year for each of the twelve Zodiac signs. And although we all realize that these forecasts can only be a general calculation for each Zodiac sign, it is for a vast majority of readers a "must read" ritual.

Astrology, however, is an ancient, serious science that dates back many thousands of years. You need to fully understand the complexities of astrology before you can interpret a natal chart, even with the help of a computer program. For this, many years of study are required.

When you have chosen a reputable astrologer, he or she will require precise details of the time, date and place of your birth. A natal chart is then drawn up for you from which the astrologer sets about the consuming task of casting your personal horoscope.

At the time you pick up your natal chart you will also receive important information about character traits that were imprinted upon you at birth, both the positive and the negative. These characteristics can remain with you throughout your destiny, shaping your actions and decisions, unless you want to work on ridding yourself of your negative aspects and strengthening your positive traits. Astrology also shows what is possible and what is probable in all aspects of your life. You will discover the career path that will give you the most satisfaction and the personality type that will bring you the most joy in marriage. The prospects of your health, wealth and happiness will be revealed, providing you with the ammunition you require to meet the challenges you are likely to encounter throughout your life. Such insight is priceless to your future well-being.

AURA READING

The technique of visualizing and interpreting auras is an advanced method of fortune telling. Some psychics are born with this ability; others have mastered the technique by frequenting psychic workshops and developing their psychic powers.

Every living thing has an energy field around it — plants, trees, animals and humans. This energy field is called an "aura", and those who can see and understand the various colors and levels of energy in the aura can predict the conditions of health, mood and spiritual evolvement of the subject it surrounds. In some psychic circles this technique is referred to as "overheading", because the reader looks only at the aura and not at the person's physical body.

The various colors of the aura reveal important information that helps the reader detect positive and negative forces affecting the subject. The aura can also reveal areas of the body which are about to be attacked by illness, as well as those that have suffered previous attacks, for instance, the sensation felt by running the hands over the aura is distinctly colder when the vibrations of a past, present or future injury — including a future car accident — is present.

Animals are very psychic beings, but they are not able to tell us where they are hurting when illness attacks them. However, a person who can read auras is equipped with the ability to detect these trouble spots by examining the aura.

The power of evil can be seen and felt in the aura of a person who is caught up in evil doings. But should they reject the lifestyle, their aura heals and is soon clearly improved.

The diagnostic skills of a psychic healer can be invaluable, for is not prevention better than cure? Those seeking the skills of a trained aura reader will be well served.

CLAIRVOYANCE AND CLAIRAUDIENCE

Most people assume that all clairvoyants enlist the aid of Tarot cards or a crystal ball to predict the future. While this is true of some, not all clairvoyants need any aids whatsoever. They have the ability to see mentally that which is invisible to the majority, like people, places and events that have passed or are yet to occur. This ability is considered a gift and is a very advanced method of fortune telling.

It is important not to confuse clairvoyance and clairaudience with Tarot card reading. While all clairvoyants and clairaudients consider themselves spiritualists, most Tarot card readers do not.

Clairaudience is the ability to hear that which is inaudible to the majority of people. Clairaudients are believed to have the ability to communicate with the dead, guardian angels, and sometimes other entities from the spirit world.

Some psychics are both clairvoyant and clairaudient, while others have just one of these gifts. A consultation with a psychic who has either or both abilities can seem awesome at first.

It is an impossible task to prove that the information given by clairvoyants and clairaudients is genuine. Frequently, however, information they have given a client about his or her past is recognized as true, and predictions for the future often prove themselves.

In this enlightened age, our minds are becoming more open and we are more inclined to believe in the sixth sense — that power of perception that can be developed into a profound psychic ability — possessed by us all.

Each of us has a valid interest in our destiny, and even when we fear it, curiosity compels us to seek answers to important questions concerning our futures. We live on a material planet, so we need to know the answers to practical, materialistic questions; as well, we are curious about what happens when we die — where do we go; will we ever see our deceased loved ones again — there are so many questions. And so we find ourselves consulting a clairvoyant who may have some of these answers.

Some people become very skeptical when a psychic who is clairaudient appears to be guessing the name of a dead relative trying to communicate with them. For instance, the psychic may ask: "Do you know someone whose name was Shane or Jane?" And you might respond: "Why not take a shot at a few more names and you might get it right." I'd like to explain how that happens.

When you consult with a psychic in this way, you open up a line of communication between the psychic and the spirit world. That line of communication becomes like a busy switchboard. You may be surprised how many souls would like to send you a message, and much like a poor telephone connection, the sound becomes muffled until the line is cleared. Hence, the apparent miscommunication. Later, of course, a message comes through which means nothing to the psychic, but which means a great deal of sense to you.

LEAD

This unusual method of fortune telling requires great skill. It is a highly potent technique, practiced by only a few psychics who claim it as their specialty and who guard the craft with great secrecy. Lead reading is reputed to be a very accurate method of fortune telling, yet it is by no means the most popular.

The process is very time-consuming. The lead is melted down. While it is still hot, it is ladled into a tub of cold water. This causes the lead to form various shapes and symbols which are interpreted by the psychic as psychic predictions.

It is a fairly common practice for lead readers to entertain their clients with a tea leaf or coffee bean reading during the lengthy melting-down period.

Caution:
There is extreme risk in handling hot lead. It should not be undertaken by anyone but an experienced practitioner.

CANDLE WAX

Predicting future events with candle wax works on the same principle as lead reading but is less complicated and less time-consuming. Two candles are lit and the hot wax is allowed to drip into a shallow dish of cold water. Small shapes and symbols form in the water and are interpreted for their psychic meaning by the person who conducts the ritual.

While the candle wax procedure is not as dangerous as the lead, it should still be undertaken with extreme care. For this reason it is wise to enlist the services of a psychic who specializes in this craft.

PSYCHOMETRY

Psychometry is a method of predicting past, present and future events by holding an object. A psychometrist interprets the impressions and symbols he or she receives while holding an object such as a piece of jewelry or an article of clothing belonging to a person who wishes to have their fortune revealed.

Anyone desirous of developing their psychic ability can practice this elementary exercise on their family or friends with adequate results. Advanced psychometrists, however, whose psychic ability is well developed, are able to quickly and accurately tune in to the events and circumstances governing the life of the object's owner.

Apart from satisfying the curiosity which lies within us all to know the details of our future, psychometry is a useful method of finding missing people — it is often used to supply information to the police which can lead to the solving of a criminal investigation. Many adopted people employ the services of a psychic who specializes in psychometry to locate their birth parents, and the police have used their services to follow the trail of an abducted person.

There are times when even the most celebrated psychometrists appear to have received mixed messages, resulting in confusion for his or her client. If you are the client, and this happens to you, don't be afraid to explain to the psychometrist that some of the information seems relevant but some information cannot possibly relate to you. There is usually a very simple explanation for this mix-up and it is this — items of jewelry which have been owned by other people will still emit vibrations relating to their former owners' destinies. Vibrations coming from such a piece could also reflect its former owner's present condition in the afterlife — a strange but interesting phenomenon. Secondhand pieces of jewelry have the same effect.

I can recall the time when a friend of mine submitted her new engagement ring to a psychometrist for a reading and the information she received promised her much long-term happiness. But there had been a history of heartbreaking events for her fiancé with a blonde female who was anything but discrete and most unfaithful. Doubt, fear, confusion, mistrust immediately engulfed her, for she had known nothing of any such previous relationship involving her fiancé. The fact that he insisted that no such relationship nor any such female had been a part of his life did little to reassure her. Instead her logic told her that if he were speaking the truth, then maybe all the good prophecies the psychometrist had given would also be untrue.

When she came to me for advice about the matter, I told her to go and ask her fiancé where he had purchased this beautiful and obviously expensive ring. Reluctantly she took my advice and the mystery was solved. Her fiancé had wanted to buy something very special for her, but could not afford it. By chance he had gone with a friend to attend the auction of a deceased person's estate, where he had purchased the ring and had it altered to fit his fiancée. It took only a little more digging and probing to discover the identity of the ring's previous owner — a blonde female who had a reputation for indulging in some pretty hedonistic behavior.

Psychometry has its own reputation for telling tales even on the deceased — whoever said "dead men don't talk" forgot about psychometry.

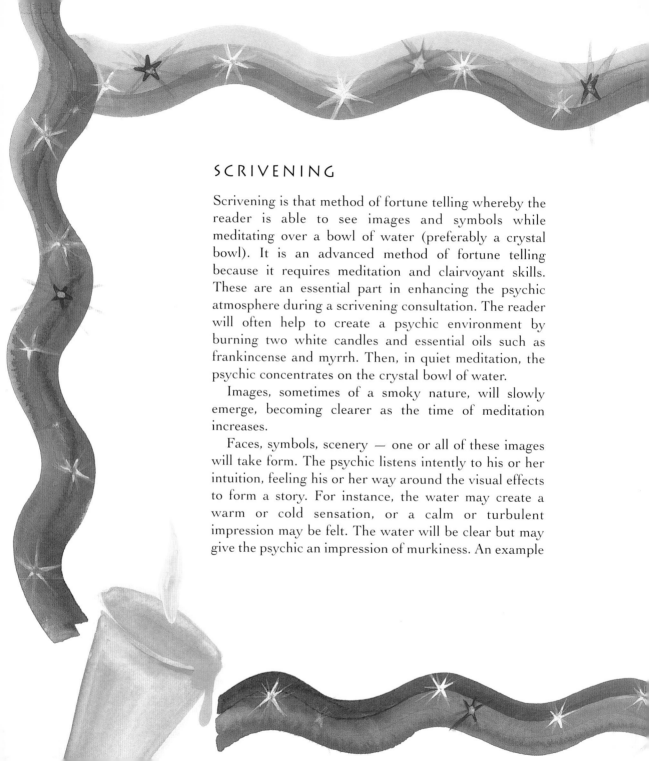

SCRIVENING

Scrivening is that method of fortune telling whereby the reader is able to see images and symbols while meditating over a bowl of water (preferably a crystal bowl). It is an advanced method of fortune telling because it requires meditation and clairvoyant skills. These are an essential part in enhancing the psychic atmosphere during a scrivening consultation. The reader will often help to create a psychic environment by burning two white candles and essential oils such as frankincense and myrrh. Then, in quiet meditation, the psychic concentrates on the crystal bowl of water.

Images, sometimes of a smoky nature, will slowly emerge, becoming clearer as the time of meditation increases.

Faces, symbols, scenery — one or all of these images will take form. The psychic listens intently to his or her intuition, feeling his or her way around the visual effects to form a story. For instance, the water may create a warm or cold sensation, or a calm or turbulent impression may be felt. The water will be clear but may give the psychic an impression of murkiness. An example

of this might be: "I see an old man (a face) causing you problems (turbulent waters) He is being dishonest about something (murky water) but things will be sorted out satisfactorily and peace will be restored (calm water).

The reason the psychic is able to interpret the signals so well is that he or she has an unrestrained mind. While this person was born with a particular sensitivity, he or she still needed to undergo rigorous training in order to achieve real results.

Scrivening is similar in practice to crystal ball gazing; it's just a case of what works best for the individual. A point that may interest you is that water signs tend to prefer scrivening, while air signs usually prefer crystal-ball gazing.

This edition published by Barnes & Noble, Inc.,
by arrangement with Lansdowne Publishing

1999 Barnes & Noble Books
Reprinted 2000

M 10 9 8 7 6 5 4 3 2

ISBN 0-7607-1224-7

Published by Lansdowne Publishing Pty Ltd
Sydney NSW 2000, Australia

Designer: Sylvie Abecassis
Illustrator: Joanna Davies

First published in 1998
© Copyright 1998 Lansdowne Publishing Pty Ltd

Set in Cochin and Lithos on QuarkXPress
Printed in Singapore by Tien Wah Press (Pte) Ltd